Narcissistic Abuse Recovery

A Practical Guide to Overcoming Codependency, Gaslighting, Complex PTSD, and Trauma

Erik Johnson

© Copyright 2024 – Erik Johnson - All rights reserved

The content within this book may not be reproduced, duplicated, or transmitted without direct written permission from the author or the publisher.

Under no circumstances will any blame or legal responsibility be held against the publisher, or author, for any damages, reparation, or monetary loss due to the information contained within this book, either directly or indirectly.

Legal Notice

This book is copyright protected. This book is only for personal use. You cannot amend, distribute, sell, use, quote, or paraphrase any part, or the content within this book, without the consent of the author-publisher.

Disclaimer Notice

Please note that the information contained within this document is for educational and entertainment purposes only. All effort has been executed to present accurate, up-to-date, and reliable, complete information. No warranties of any kind are declared or implied. Readers acknowledge that the author is not engaging in the rendering of legal, financial, medical, or professional advice.

Table of Content

Introduction 6

Chapter 1: Navigating the Landscape 8

Narcissisticm Abuse: Understanding Its Definition, Manifestations, and Real-Life Examples 8

Complex PTSD: Overview, Symptoms, and Triggers Linked to Abuse 11

Chapter 2: Untangling the Web of Codependency and Narcissism 13

Understanding Why Codependents Are Drawn to Narcissists 13

The Cycle of Narcissistic Abuse: From Idealization to Discarding 13

Personal Stories: John's Journey from Codependency to Self-Awareness 14

Key Steps to Recovery 16

Chapter 3: Narcissism Across Different Relationships 19

Narcissism in Romantic Relationships 19

Narcissism in Family Relationships 20

Friendships and Narcissism 20

Narcissism in the Workplace 21

Chapter 4: Understanding Gaslighting and Its Impacts 24

Examples of Gaslighting in Action 24

Emotional and Cognitive Effects of Gaslighting 25

Tools for Self-Assessment: Identifying Signs of Gaslighting 25

Chapter 5: The Shadows of Complex PTSD 28

Recognizing the Symptoms of Complex PTSD from Prolonged Abuse 28

Survivor Narratives 28

Linking Abuse to C-PTSD: Understanding Manipulative Behaviors 29

Chapter 6: Practical Approaches to Healing and Recovery 32

Self-Awareness: Validating Your Feelings and Experiences 32

Understanding Narcissistic Abuse: Recognizing It's Not Your Fault 32

Facing the Backlash After Cutting Ties 33

Allowing Yourself to Grieve the Relationship 34

Selecting the Right Therapist for Trauma and Narcissistic Abuse Recovery 35

Key Questions to Ask a Potential Therapist 35

Support Groups: Joining Communities for Narcissistic Abuse Survivors 36

Family and Friends: Educating Loved Ones About Narcissistic Abuse 37

Journaling: A Tool for Emotional Processing and Progress Tracking 37

Promoting Independence Through Engaging Activities 39

Chapter 7: Establishing Boundaries and Nurturing Self-Love 41

Practical Advice on Setting Healthy Boundaries with Real-Life Examples 41

Strategies for Upholding Boundaries 42

Techniques for Cultivating Self-Love and Self-Compassion 43

Daily Affirmations and Journaling 44

The Importance of Self-Care Routines and How to Establish Them 46

Chapter 8: Building Healthy Relationships 49

Defining a Healthy Relationship: Key Characteristics and Foundations 49

Recognizing Red Flags in Relationships 50

Anecdote for a Romantic Relationship: 51

Chapter 9: Moving Forward 54

Sustaining Progress and Managing Setbacks 54

Redefining Your Identity and Future 55

Chapter 10: Embracing Empowerment and Self-Advocacy.................. 57

The Power of Self-Advocacy 57

Creating a Vision for the Future 59

Embracing Lifelong Learning and Self-Discovery 60

Transforming Pain into Purpose: The Power of Personal Narrative 61

Chapter 11: Forging New Paths and Living Authentically 64

Letting Go of the Past: Releasing the Hold of Abuse 64

Embracing New Opportunities: Redefining Your Life on Your Own Terms 65

Authenticity: Living in Alignment with Your True Self 65
Resilience in the Face of Adversity: Navigating Future Challenges 66
Embracing Your Power as a Lifelong Journey 68
Giving Back: Turning Your Journey into a Source of Strength for Others 69
Living a Life Rooted in Your Values 70
Conclusion **72**

Introduction

When I first set out to understand and recover from narcissistic abuse, I never anticipated that it would lead me to write this book. My drive to create it comes from both my personal experience and the countless stories I've heard from others who have faced similar struggles. Having gone through the process of healing myself, I deeply understand the far-reaching effects that narcissistic abuse can have on someone's life.

In my early twenties, I was in what appeared to be an ideal relationship. However, after a few months, I began to notice subtle but damaging patterns of control and manipulation. Gaslighting, emotional abuse, and the gradual breakdown of my self-esteem left lasting marks. It took time, therapy, and the unwavering support of those close to me to regain my sense of identity and rebuild my life. I am fortunate to have recognized the toxicity early enough to escape before even greater harm was done, but I know that not everyone is as lucky, and my heart goes out to you.

This book is an attempt to share the insights and methods that have aided my recovery and that of many others. Drawing upon

Summary of Key Topics and Reader Takeaways

In the upcoming chapters, we will dive into the complex world of narcissistic abuse and the steps toward recovery. We begin by exploring the nature of narcissism across various relationships—whether in romantic partnerships, family connections, friendships, or professional settings. You'll learn to identify the subtle and manipulative tactics narcissists employ, such as gaslighting, with real-life examples to help you recognize these behaviors more clearly.

Next, we shift focus to the healing journey. Topics like setting firm boundaries and fostering self-compassion are emphasized, with actionable recovery strategies laid out in detail. These include therapy options, mindfulness practices, and self-care routines. Through a blend of personal stories and expert advice, you will receive the support and guidance necessary for your own path to recovery.

Encouragement for Your Healing and Self-Discovery Journey

Starting the journey to recover from narcissistic abuse can be both difficult and deeply transformative. This book is meant to be your companion, offering not only practical tools and insights but also encouragement. Healing is unique to each person, so allow yourself the freedom to move at your own pace. As you engage with the chapters, take time to reflect, apply the strategies, and celebrate even the smallest victories.

You are far from alone on this path. Many others have faced similar challenges and emerged stronger and more empowered. With the right resources and support, you too can reclaim your life and create a future filled with happiness, peace, and fulfillment.

Chapter 1:
Navigating the Landscape

In the complex world of human relationships, interactions sometimes veer into darker territory, where manipulation and control take hold, casting a long shadow through behaviors like narcissistic abuse and gaslighting. This chapter unpacks these destructive dynamics, offering insight into their mechanisms, their far-reaching consequences, and the pervasive damage they leave behind.

Narcissisticm Abuse: Understanding Its Definition, Manifestations, and Real-Life Examples

Narcissism, as defined by psychologists, goes beyond simple selfishness or self-centeredness. It involves a deeply rooted sense of superiority, a relentless need for admiration, and a profound lack of empathy. Narcissists exhibit this personality disorder through manipulative behaviors, aimed at inflating their ego, often at the expense of others. They are typically charming on the surface, which conceals their more self-serving and controlling tendencies, making their harmful actions especially insidious.

At the core of narcissistic abuse is a powerful desire to dominate others—emotionally, physically, and mentally. Narcissists don't just seek control for its own sake; they aim to reshape their partner's reality, bending it to fulfill their own emotional needs while ignoring the damage inflicted. This abuse can take many forms, including tactics that subtly dismantle the victim's self-worth and distort their perception of reality. It often begins with minor criticisms, which gradually escalate into a full-scale attack on the victim's confidence and mental clarity.

For example, Samara shares her experience of being married for ten years to a man who constantly undermined her every decision. "It felt like I was living in a fog, never fully understanding why I felt so small," she recalls. Her story is a classic example of narcissistic manipulation, as her husband employed tactics like belittling her opinions, humiliating her in public, and slowly isolating her from loved ones. This isolation made her increasingly reliant on him for emotional and social validation, which in turn made her easier to control.

As Dr. Ramani Durvasula, a leading expert on narcissism, notes, "Narcissistic abuse often begins so subtly that the fog of confusion creeps in unnoticed until you're completely lost in it." This "fog" describes the disorienting mental state that narcissistic tactics create—where victims begin to doubt their own thoughts, emotions, and memories. Narcissists commonly use strategies such as belittling, name-calling, and gaslighting to further cloud their victim's judgment. They often twist the narrative, portraying themselves as the victim to avoid accountability, leaving their partner isolated and confused. Over time, these manipulative patterns strip the victim of self-esteem and mental clarity, making them question their own reality and sanity.

This cyclical abuse serves the narcissist's unrelenting need for control and validation. It ensures they remain at the center of the relationship while diminishing their partner into a state of submission and emotional dependence. The long-term effects of such relationships can be devastating, undermining one's self-identity and trust, and requiring significant time and effort to heal.

Gaslighting: Understanding the Concept, Recognizing the Signs, and Its Psychological Impact

Gaslighting, a term originating from the 1944 film *Gaslight*, in which a husband manipulates his wife into questioning her sanity, represents a particularly insidious form of psychological abuse. This form of manipulation occurs when an abuser denies the victim's reality so consistently and convincingly that the victim begins to doubt their own perceptions, memories, and even mental stability.

Gaslighting typically starts subtly, with the abuser denying or twisting minor facts, which gradually escalates into more severe distortions of reality. Over time, victims may begin to second-guess themselves, becoming increasingly dependent on the gaslighter for their version of events. This psychological manipulation often leaves victims feeling disoriented, powerless, and unable to trust their own judgment.

Research published in the *Journal of Interpersonal Violence* indicates that many survivors of intimate partner violence report experiencing gaslighting, highlighting how widespread this tactic is in abusive relationships. The emotional and psychological effects of gaslighting are profound, often resulting in low self-esteem, anxiety, depression, and challenges in future relationships.

For instance, Emily, a gaslighting victim, once questioned why her partner didn't call when he was late. His sharp response, "You're crazy! I told you yesterday I'd be late," left Emily doubting her memory. Over time, she began apologizing for things she hadn't done, just to maintain peace. This constant undermining of her reality is a textbook example of gaslighting, which gradually eroded her confidence and sense of self.

Gaslighting extends beyond personal relationships and can occur in workplaces, where power dynamics are manipulated, or even in political contexts to sway opinions and suppress dissent. Its power lies in the abuser's ability to distort truth and evade accountability.

To combat gaslighting, it's essential to recognize the signs, seek support, and, if needed, pursue professional help to rebuild confidence in one's perceptions. By identifying gaslighting, victims can begin to reclaim their sense of reality and break free from the control of those who manipulate them.

Codependency: Traits, Origins, and Its Role in Dysfunctional Relationships

Codependency is a behavioral pattern that often originates in early family dynamics, leading individuals to seek approval and validation from others, particularly in intimate relationships. Those affected by codependency tend to fear rejection, which drives an unhealthy reliance on others for emotional stability and self-worth.

Dr. Lisa Firestone describes codependency as a "dance of avoidance," where individuals distract themselves from their own unresolved pain by focusing excessively on another person's needs and challenges. This behavior often creates an ideal environment for relationships with narcissists, who thrive on the codependent's need for approval. The codependent partner becomes deeply entrenched in the narcissist's manipulative behavior, gradually losing their sense of autonomy and self-worth.

In such relationships, the codependent's emotional well-being becomes tied to the narcissist's whims, often resulting in a cycle of emotional imbalance and dissatisfaction. The more a codependent partner seeks validation, the more the narcissist exploits their vulnerabilities, intensifying the destructive dynamic. Over time, the codependent person's sense of self erodes, and they find it increasingly difficult to break free from the relationship.

Understanding the roots and traits of codependency is crucial in addressing these dynamics. By focusing on self-awareness, setting boundaries, and seeking therapeutic support, codependent individuals can regain their independence and cultivate healthier relationships.

Complex PTSD: Overview, Symptoms, and Triggers Linked to Abuse

Complex Post-Traumatic Stress Disorder (C-PTSD) develops from prolonged exposure to sustained traumatic experiences, often seen in individuals subjected to narcissistic abuse. Unlike traditional PTSD, which typically arises from a single traumatic event, C-PTSD stems from ongoing, inescapable trauma. Those affected by C-PTSD frequently struggle with persistent symptoms such as recurring nightmares, emotional detachment, and deep mistrust of others.

Dr. Judith Herman first introduced the concept of C-PTSD in the 1990s, emphasizing how it differs from PTSD. Survivors of C-PTSD experience more complex psychological effects, including difficulty regulating emotions, a skewed sense of self-worth, and the pervasive belief that safety and trust are unattainable.

One poignant example comes from James, a survivor of narcissistic abuse, who compares his recovery process to learning how to walk again after years of being confined. He describes the ongoing struggle with intense flashbacks, overwhelming anxiety, and an ever-present fear of "falling" back into the emotional and psychological chaos of his past. James's inability to trust others, even those with good intentions, kept him isolated and emotionally distant. Emotional numbness also stripped away his ability to connect with loved ones or find joy in activities that once fulfilled him. His story encapsulates the deep, enduring nature of C-PTSD, demonstrating how it impacts not just emotions but the very essence of a survivor's ability to function in everyday life.

In this chapter, we have explored the intricate dynamics of narcissistic abuse by breaking down essential concepts such as narcissism, codependency, Complex PTSD (C-PTSD), and gaslighting. Understanding these elements is key to recognizing how they intertwine to create a toxic and manipulative environment.

Narcissists typically display behaviors rooted in grandiosity, a lack of empathy, and an unquenchable need for admiration. Codependent individuals, on the other hand, often exhibit excessive caregiving tendencies and a deep fear of abandonment, making them vulnerable to narcissistic manipulation. The chapter also delved into gaslighting, where abusers manipulate their victims into doubting their own reality, and the long-term psychological toll this tactic can take. C-PTSD, triggered by prolonged abuse, manifests through emotional dysregulation, hypervigilance, and the overwhelming difficulty of regaining control over one's life.

By recognizing these patterns and behaviors, survivors can gain clarity about their experiences and take the first steps toward healing. Setting boundaries, engaging in therapy, and building strong support networks are critical tools in recovering from the deep scars of narcissistic abuse.

As you continue your journey toward healing, remember that understanding these complex dynamics is a vital first step in reclaiming your sense of self. With knowledge, support, and resilience, it is entirely possible to recover from narcissistic abuse, build healthier relationships, and ultimately thrive. Though challenging, the path to healing is within reach for those who are determined to overcome the lasting effects of abuse.

Chapter 2:
Untangling the Web of Codependency and Narcissism

Few relationship dynamics are as intricate and destructive as the interaction between codependency and narcissism. What often begins as a seemingly perfect and intense bond can quickly deteriorate into cycles of control, manipulation, and emotional harm. This chapter aims to explore the psychological roots of both codependency and narcissism, offering insights into why these traits attract one another and how to break free from the damaging patterns they create.

Understanding Why Codependents Are Drawn to Narcissists

At first glance, it may seem surprising that codependent individuals are often attracted to narcissists. However, when we delve deeper into the psychological profiles of both personalities, the attraction begins to make sense. Codependents, who often harbor a deep need for validation and approval, may be drawn to the apparent strength and confidence that narcissists exude. To the emotionally vulnerable, the narcissist's charisma and assertiveness can seem like the answer to their insecurities, creating a false sense of safety.

Dr. Ramani Durvasula explains that codependents may misinterpret a narcissist's assertiveness as emotional stability, making them believe that their partner's confidence will provide protection from their own fears of rejection and abandonment. This dynamic sets the stage for a toxic relationship, where the codependent person seeks approval and the narcissist thrives on admiration and control. Understanding this dynamic is key to unraveling the emotional vulnerabilities that perpetuate such relationships.

The Cycle of Narcissistic Abuse: From Idealization to Discarding

The cycle of narcissistic abuse typically follows a predictable pattern, moving from idealization to devaluation and, eventually, discarding. Emma's story provides a clear example of this progression. Initially, she was swept off her feet by her partner's charm, grand gestures, and intense affection during the *idealization* phase. Narcissists often employ love-bombing tactics, showering their partners with praise, gifts, and attention to create an illusion of a perfect relationship.

However, as the relationship continued, the *devaluation* phase began to surface. Her partner started to criticize and manipulate her, chipping away at her self-esteem. This phase is marked by gaslighting, shifting blame, and emotional abuse, leaving the victim feeling confused and desperate for the narcissist's approval. Emma became increasingly dependent on her partner's validation, even as her sense of self deteriorated.

Eventually, Emma's partner moved into the *discarding* phase, where he withdrew emotionally and ended the relationship. Narcissists often discard their partners when they no longer serve as a source of narcissistic supply—once the admiration and control diminish, they lose interest. For victims like Emma, this phase can be devastating, as they are left grappling with feelings of worthlessness and confusion. However, it also represents an opportunity for healing and recovery, as the end of the relationship can serve as the first step toward reclaiming one's identity.

Emma's journey highlights the psychological tactics used by narcissists at each stage of the abuse cycle, offering a deeper understanding of the emotional roller coaster that victims endure. Recognizing these patterns is critical to breaking free from the toxic dynamics and beginning the path to recovery.

Personal Stories: John's Journey from Codependency to Self-Awareness

John's experience with a narcissistic partner provides another powerful illustration of the codependent-narcissist dynamic. Early in his relationship with Mara, John was captivated by her charm and the attention she showered on him. However, over time, that affection shifted to control and criticism, leaving John feeling increasingly inadequate. His constant need to please Mara—a deeply ingrained codependent trait—only made him more vulnerable to her manipulative tactics.

It wasn't until John sought therapy that he first encountered the concept of codependency. This realization was the turning point in his journey. He began to understand how his fear of rejection had trapped him in a relationship where his self-worth was entirely dependent on Mara's approval. As he gained more insight into narcissistic behavior, John recognized the gaslighting and manipulation Mara used to maintain control over him.

John's recovery was slow and painful, filled with moments of isolation and sadness as he distanced himself from the toxic relationship. However, his story is also one of hope and transformation. Through therapy and self-reflection, John gradually rebuilt his sense of self, learning to establish boundaries and seek healthier connections. His journey serves as a testament to the possibility of growth and healing, even after years of emotional entanglement with a narcissist.

John's story, shared in therapy groups and wellness workshops, has inspired others in similar situations, offering a message of resilience and the importance of self-awareness. His experience demonstrates that, while the path to recovery is challenging, it is also filled with opportunities for personal growth and the reclaiming of one's life.

The interplay between codependency and narcissism forms a toxic and often destructive relationship dynamic. Codependent individuals, seeking validation and fearful of rejection, are drawn to the confidence and control that narcissists present. In turn, narcissists exploit these vulnerabilities to maintain dominance, perpetuating a cycle of emotional abuse that erodes the codependent partner's sensc of self.

Through the personal stories of Emma and John, we have explored the phases of narcissistic abuse and the journey toward healing. Understanding the stages of idealization, devaluation, and discarding, as well as recognizing one's own codependent tendencies, is essential for breaking free from these damaging relationships.

This chapter has laid the groundwork for identifying the patterns of codependency and narcissism, offering insights and strategies for recovery. By developing self-awareness, seeking therapy, and establishing boundaries, those caught in the web of codependency and narcissism can begin to foster healthier, more balanced connections and ultimately reclaim their sense of identity and self-worth.

Pathways to Healing: Mapping the Road to Recovery

Recovering from harmful relationships requires a well-structured and intentional approach. Recognizing the early signs of toxic behavior, setting strong personal boundaries, and engaging in therapeutic practices are key steps in this process. Psychologists emphasize the importance of rebuilding self-esteem and cultivating respectful, healthy relationships. This guidance helps individuals rediscover their self-worth and confidently assert their needs, creating a foundation for lasting emotional resilience.

Key Steps to Recovery

- **Identifying Early Signs of Toxic Behavior**
- Recognizing toxic behaviors early is essential for self-protection. Common red flags include manipulation, constant disrespect, and controlling behaviors. Being able to identify these patterns helps individuals take proactive steps to protect their well-being.
- **Establishing Firm Personal Boundaries**
- Boundaries serve as a crucial defense against toxic influences, ensuring that one's emotional needs are prioritized. This includes clearly communicating limits and standing firm against behaviors that threaten emotional safety. Setting and maintaining boundaries is fundamental to fostering emotional health and security.
- **Therapeutic Methods for Recovery**
- Therapy plays a significant role in the recovery process. Approaches like Cognitive-Behavioral Therapy (CBT), Dialectical Behavior Therapy (DBT), and trauma-focused therapy offer effective ways to process past trauma, develop healthy coping strategies, and build emotional resilience.
- **Reconstructing Self-Esteem**
- Experts recommend engaging in self-affirming activities, setting achievable goals, and surrounding oneself with supportive people. These actions help individuals regain

confidence and create a positive self-image, which is crucial for long-term healing.
- **Promoting Healthy, Respectful Relationships**
- Developing healthy relationships involves recognizing key qualities such as mutual respect, clear communication, and emotional support. Psychologists stress the importance of connecting with people who respect your boundaries and encourage personal growth, ensuring that relationships are built on trust and respect.
- **Expert Insights and Practical Guidance**
- Guidance from experts helps individuals navigate the complexities of toxic relationships, providing actionable steps to rebuild their lives. This expert advice is crucial for creating new, healthier dynamics in future relationships.

The ultimate goal of these healing pathways is to foster enduring emotional resilience. By learning to identify toxic behaviors, establish boundaries, engage in therapy, and nurture healthy relationships, individuals can rediscover their self-worth and confidently assert their needs. Later chapters will dive deeper into these topics, offering additional tools for recovering from narcissistic abuse.

The complex dynamic of codependency and narcissism creates a toxic cycle of manipulation and emotional harm. This chapter has explored the key traits of both codependent and narcissistic individuals, showing how their interactions fuel a destructive pattern. By understanding these dynamics, survivors can begin to break free from these harmful patterns.

Codependency often stems from early family environments, leading to an unhealthy dependence on others for approval and identity. Narcissists, on the other hand, thrive on control and admiration, exploiting the vulnerabilities of the codependent. This relationship pattern can cause deep emotional damage, leaving individuals feeling worthless, stressed, and disconnected from their true selves.

However, with expert insights and strategies—such as setting boundaries, seeking therapy, and practicing self-care—there is hope for recovery. The personal stories shared in this chapter highlight the possibility of healing and emphasize the importance of self-awareness and community support.

As you continue your journey, remember that with knowledge, support, and perseverance, you can overcome these toxic patterns and build healthier, more fulfilling relationships. While recovery is a challenging process, the right tools and guidance make it entirely achievable.

Chapter 3:
Narcissism Across Different Relationships

Narcissism can deeply affect various types of relationships, leaving emotional damage and disrupting the lives of those involved. This chapter explores how narcissistic behavior appears in romantic relationships, family settings, friendships, and the workplace. By examining these different scenarios, readers can better understand how narcissism impacts relationships and learn to identify the signs early.

Narcissism in Romantic Relationships

Previously, we discussed how narcissists discard their victims in romantic relationships, but here, we will look at a slightly different scenario. Narcissism in romantic relationships often begins with intense charm and admiration, where the narcissist idealizes their partner. This phase is marked by grand romantic gestures and promises of a flawless future, creating a fairy-tale-like experience. However, as the relationship progresses, the narcissist's behavior typically shifts dramatically.

Take Sarah and Tom, for example. In the beginning, Tom was incredibly charming, surprising Sarah with extravagant dates and constant admiration. But as time passed, Tom's behavior changed. He began to criticize Sarah over minor issues and isolated her from friends and family, disguising his control as care and protection. His affection turned to manipulation, using gaslighting to make Sarah doubt her own reality. He denied hurtful comments and dismissed her feelings as overreactions.

As Tom's control grew stronger, Sarah's self-esteem eroded, and the relationship became a source of emotional pain. Eventually, Sarah found the strength to leave, recognizing the toxic cycle—a difficult but necessary step towards healing.

Narcissism in Family Relationships

Narcissism within families often takes complex forms, typically involving one or more members who exert control and manipulation. A common example is seen in the Johnson family, where Mr. Johnson displays strong narcissistic traits. He favors his eldest son, Michael, who is constantly praised and held in high regard, creating a "golden child" dynamic. While Michael may develop an inflated sense of self-importance and struggle with criticism, he may also feel immense pressure to live up to his father's unrealistic standards, leading to emotional strain.

In contrast, Michael's sister, Lisa, is cast as the "scapegoat," blamed for the family's issues and unfairly punished for minor mistakes. As a result, Lisa grows up struggling with low self-worth and self-doubt, constantly questioning her value. Though children like Lisa often face significant emotional challenges, they can eventually reclaim their sense of self-worth once they break free from such a toxic family environment. However, this often requires overcoming intense guilt and shame inflicted by these dysfunctional dynamics.

Mrs. Johnson, the enabling parent, overlooks Mr. Johnson's harmful behavior to avoid conflict, dismissing her children's concerns as overreactions. This lack of acknowledgment only perpetuates the unhealthy family dynamic, causing lasting emotional harm to all members. By exploring these roles in depth, we aim to shed light on the long-term effects of narcissistic family dynamics and offer insights into possible paths for recovery and personal growth for those affected.

Friendships and Narcissism

In friendships, narcissism often creates an unbalanced dynamic where the narcissist demands constant attention and admiration while failing to offer genuine support in return. These relationships may begin on a positive note, built around shared interests and engaging activities, but eventually reveal a more self-centered pattern.

For instance, consider Natalie and Jenna's friendship, which blossomed after meeting in a photography class. They bonded quickly over their mutual love of art, spending time exploring galleries and sharing creative ideas. In the beginning, Jenna appeared to be an empathetic and supportive friend, often initiating deep conversations about life goals and challenges.

However, as their friendship deepened, Natalie noticed that Jenna frequently shifted conversations back to herself, disregarding Natalie's perspectives and experiences. Jenna's initial attentiveness transformed into a constant need for validation and support, with little reciprocation for Natalie's emotional needs. Over time, Natalie found herself playing the role of a passive listener rather than an equal participant.

The friendship deteriorated further when Jenna reacted negatively to Natalie's successes and minimized her problems. This behavior is typical of narcissistic individuals, who prioritize their own emotional validation over the needs of others. What began as a mutually enjoyable friendship evolved into a one-sided relationship, leaving Natalie feeling undervalued and frustrated as her self-esteem was gradually diminished by Jenna's self-centered behavior.

Narcissism in the Workplace

In professional environments, narcissism can disrupt workplace harmony, particularly when exhibited by a colleague or supervisor. Narcissistic bosses, in particular, often use their authority to exploit employees, seeking recognition and power at the expense of team morale and cohesion.

Consider Mr. Stevens, a charismatic leader who initially won the admiration of his staff with his visionary ideas and assertive leadership style. His charm and dynamic approach garnered loyalty from his team, who believed in his ambitious plans. However, over time, the darker side of Mr. Stevens' personality began to emerge. He expected unwavering loyalty, demanding that employees prioritize his directives above their well-being or professional judgment.

Mr. Stevens also took credit for the ideas and hard work of his team members, presenting them as his own in important meetings. When confronted with constructive criticism, he reacted by subtly punishing dissenters—reducing their responsibilities, excluding them from key projects, or publicly humiliating them. Moreover, Mr.

Stevens cultivated a competitive atmosphere, pitting employees against one another in the belief that competition would drive productivity. Instead, this created an insecure and divisive environment, where trust eroded, and collaboration was replaced by suspicion and rivalry.

This example highlights how a narcissistic leader can initially appear as a transformative figure, but gradually reveal their manipulative and self-serving tendencies. Such behavior not only affects team dynamics but also undermines employee satisfaction and performance.

Recognizing how narcissism manifests in different types of relationships is vital for understanding its far-reaching impacts. This chapter has explored narcissism in romantic partnerships, friendships, family dynamics, and the workplace, demonstrating how this personality disorder can infiltrate various aspects of life.

In romantic relationships, narcissism often begins with idealization, followed by a phase of devaluation, and finally, discard, leaving partners emotionally drained and manipulated. In friendships, the narcissist demands constant validation while offering little in return, creating one-sided interactions that diminish the other person's self-worth. Lastly, in the workplace, narcissism can disrupt team cohesion and morale, as narcissistic leaders manipulate colleagues and take credit for others' efforts. Recognizing these behaviors is the first step toward addressing and mitigating the damage caused by narcissistic individuals across different relationships.

Within families, narcissistic dynamics can be especially harmful, as they often assign roles like the golden child and scapegoat, which lead to enduring psychological damage. Narcissistic parents exert control and manipulation, while enabling parents may excuse or ignore the toxic behavior, further entrenching the dysfunction. Children growing up in these environments often face challenges with self-esteem and identity, which can hinder their personal development well into adulthood.

In the workplace, narcissistic behavior from bosses or colleagues creates toxic atmospheres characterized by manipulation, exploitation, and the undermining of others. This behavior fosters a culture of fear and competition, damaging both team cohesion and individual well-being.

Experts and real-life stories emphasize the importance of identifying these toxic patterns early and taking proactive steps to safeguard one's mental health. Setting clear boundaries, seeking professional support, and developing strong support networks are crucial strategies for recovery and building long-term resilience.

Chapter 4:
Understanding Gaslighting and Its Impacts

In this chapter, we will delve into the mechanisms of gaslighting, a form of psychological abuse that deeply affects emotional and cognitive well-being. By examining real-life scenarios and expert insights, we aim to equip readers with the knowledge to recognize and resist gaslighting, ultimately helping them regain their sense of self and reality.

Examples of Gaslighting in Action

Gaslighting is a manipulative tactic that erodes an individual's grasp on reality. Here, we'll explore some common techniques used by gaslighters through detailed scenarios. These examples reveal how manipulators use deception to create confusion, fostering doubt and dependency in their victims.

Scenario 1: Denying Conversations or Events

Imagine Jade, who frequently hears her partner, Henry, make hurtful remarks. When she confronts him, Henry flatly denies ever saying those things, insisting Jade is either misremembering or being overly sensitive. Over time, Jade begins to doubt her memory and questions whether she's overreacting, gradually losing confidence in her own perceptions.

Scenario 2: Spreading False Narratives of Untrustworthiness

In another case, Marcus's colleague, Alison, tells him that their coworkers find him unreliable and erratic. Alison often "forgets" to invite Marcus to important meetings and then blames him for falling behind on tasks. Isolated and dependent on Alison for key information, Marcus starts believing her narrative and loses faith in his own competence.

These examples illustrate the calculated tactics gaslighters use to destabilize their victims by distorting their perception of reality and isolating them, making the victim increasingly reliant on the manipulator.

Emotional and Cognitive Effects of Gaslighting

The emotional and cognitive toll of enduring gaslighting can be profound and long-lasting. Victims often experience chronic anxiety and depressive symptoms as a result of continuously doubting their perceptions and memories. This emotional distress stems from the ongoing manipulation, which chips away at their sense of reality and self-confidence.

Prolonged exposure to gaslighting can also lead to **Complex PTSD (C-PTSD)**, a condition that leaves individuals with heightened anxiety, recurring nightmares, and a pervasive mistrust of others. This mistrust makes it difficult for victims to form or maintain healthy relationships, further isolating them.

From a cognitive standpoint, gaslighting creates severe **cognitive dissonance**, leaving victims unsure of what is real or imagined. This confusion impairs decision-making and diminishes their ability to trust their own thoughts. Over time, the sustained mental strain can disrupt cognitive function, leading to significant challenges in both personal and professional settings.

The cumulative effect of gaslighting can lead to long-term damage to mental health, causing lasting difficulties with self-esteem, decision-making, and overall emotional stability. Recognizing and addressing these effects is crucial for recovery and rebuilding one's sense of self.

Tools for Self-Assessment: Identifying Signs of Gaslighting

To assist individuals in recognizing gaslighting behaviors, the following checklist provides a practical self-assessment tool based on key psychological principles:

Gaslighting Self-Assessment Checklist:

1. **Reality Questioning:**
   - Do you often question whether events you remember actually happened?
   - Are you frequently unsure if your feelings and reactions are valid?
2. **Confusion and Doubt:**
   - Do you feel more confused and less confident than before your relationship began?
   - Are you constantly second-guessing your thoughts and decisions?
3. **Feeling "Crazy":**
   - Does the person regularly tell you that you're imagining things or acting irrationally?
   - Do you feel as if you might be losing your sanity?
4. **Isolation from Support:**
   - Has your relationship distanced you from family and friends?
   - Are you discouraged from seeing others or told that they are bad influences?
5. **Apologizing Reluctantly:**
   - Do you find yourself apologizing even when you feel you've done nothing wrong?
   - Are you expected to apologize even when the fault lies with the other person?
6. **Deflecting Responsibility:**
   - Does the person refuse to take responsibility for hurtful actions or words?
   - Are you blamed for their behaviors or the negative outcomes they cause?
7. **Withholding Information:**
   - Do they withhold information, making you feel uninformed or inferior?
   - Do you feel intentionally left out of important discussions or decisions?
8. **Twisting and Reframing:**
   - When you express concerns, are your words twisted or used against you?
   - Do your statements get reframed to make you seem selfish or unreasonable?

This checklist is designed to help individuals identify patterns of gaslighting in their interactions. Recognizing these signs is a key step in addressing the situation, seeking help, and regaining control over one's life.

Conclusion

Recognizing gaslighting is crucial for reclaiming one's sense of reality and self-worth after experiencing narcissistic abuse. In this chapter, we have explored how gaslighting techniques—such as denying events, twisting words, and manipulating perceptions—undermine a victim's sense of self.

We also examined the emotional and cognitive effects of gaslighting, including confusion, self-doubt, and chronic anxiety. Survivor stories provided real-life examples of the profound impact these tactics can have, while expert insights emphasized the importance of education and self-awareness in combating this form of abuse.

Moving forward, awareness is the first step toward healing. By acknowledging the red flags of gaslighting and seeking support from those who validate your experiences, you can begin to rebuild your sense of reality. Techniques such as journaling, mindfulness, and therapy are valuable tools for restoring emotional stability and strengthening your self-confidence.

Recovery from gaslighting is a continuous journey, but with resilience and self-trust, you can overcome these manipulative behaviors and thrive beyond the shadows of psychological abuse.

Chapter 5:
The Shadows of Complex PTSD

Complex PTSD (C-PTSD) casts long, persistent shadows on the lives of those who endure it, often stemming from repeated trauma such as narcissistic abuse. Unlike traditional PTSD, which is typically triggered by a singular traumatic event, C-PTSD arises from prolonged, inescapable trauma that deeply affects an individual's psychological state. In this chapter, we will explore the complexity of C-PTSD, detailing its symptoms, the underlying causes, and potential pathways for understanding and healing.

Recognizing the Symptoms of Complex PTSD from Prolonged Abuse

To understand C-PTSD, it's essential to recognize the wide range of emotional and psychological challenges it presents. In addition to chronic feelings of emptiness and emotional dysregulation—often expressed as unpredictable anger or intense sadness—C-PTSD is marked by dissociative symptoms. These can include a sense of detachment from one's life or surroundings and vivid flashbacks of past trauma. Other symptoms include severe sleep disturbances, heightened vigilance, and an exaggerated startle response to everyday stimuli.

These symptoms are not isolated occurrences but the result of ongoing emotional and mental strain caused by extended periods of abuse. Environments dominated by manipulative behaviors, such as narcissistic abuse and gaslighting, perpetuate the mental toll, leaving lasting impacts on the victim's emotional health.

Survivor Narratives

Kelly's Story: Kelly recalls feeling a deep sense of emptiness, with daily episodes of overwhelming sadness and anger sparked by seemingly minor triggers. She also frequently experienced flashbacks, reliving traumatic moments from her past as if they were happening in real time, leaving her feeling powerless and distressed.

Jonathan's Story: Jonathan describes his life under the constant pressure of hypervigilance. Every sudden noise or unexpected movement triggered intense anxiety, a leftover effect from his years of heightened alertness to avoid conflicts with his abusive partner. His nights were filled with nightmares, leaving him exhausted and anxious as each day began.

These survivor narratives reveal the inescapable impact of C-PTSD on daily life. They show how chronic emotional abuse, control, and stress lead to deep-seated psychological wounds. The stories also emphasize the need for therapeutic approaches that address the unique complexities of C-PTSD, offering paths toward healing from the underlying trauma.

Linking Abuse to C-PTSD: Understanding Manipulative Behaviors

The link between narcissistic abuse, gaslighting, and the development of C-PTSD is well-established in psychological research. Prolonged manipulative behaviors erode the victim's sense of identity and reality, key factors in the onset of this disorder. Experts such as Dr. Judith Herman have highlighted how these behaviors disrupt the victim's self-concept and alter stress response mechanisms, impairing emotional regulation and the ability to feel safe.

Chronic stress and emotional control are major contributors to C-PTSD. Studies show that people exposed to long-term psychological abuse exhibit elevated levels of cortisol, the body's stress hormone. This ongoing stress response can alter brain structure and function, impairing the victim's ability to regulate emotions and feel secure. The constant erosion of self-worth and persistent feelings of powerlessness further aggravate these effects, creating a strong foundation for the development of C-PTSD.

Both empirical data and theoretical insights emphasize how sustained emotional manipulation and the gradual destruction of self-esteem lead to chronic stress, which plays a critical role in C-PTSD. By examining case studies and clinical observations, psychologists have drawn clear connections between these abusive behaviors and the psychological symptoms of C-PTSD. Understanding this link is essential for designing effective therapeutic strategies that address the root causes of trauma, helping survivors move toward lasting recovery.

Voices of Resilience: Jessica's Journey from Manipulation to Empowerment

In this section, we hear from survivors like Jessica, who share their powerful stories of transformation. Jessica's decades-long marriage was dominated by her husband's narcissistic manipulation, where her decisions, emotions, and even memories were constantly undermined. Over time, she began to notice discrepancies between her recollections and her husband's version of events. This persistent doubt led her to explore psychological manipulation, where she first encountered the term "gaslighting." This discovery marked a pivotal moment in her journey.

Realizing that her struggles were the result of long-term emotional abuse, Jessica took bold steps toward reclaiming her life. She sought therapy that specialized in narcissistic abuse, joined support groups where she connected with others facing similar challenges, and learned to set firm personal boundaries. Her path to recovery was not without difficulty—filled with moments of doubt, but also triumph. Through external support and her determination to change, Jessica transitioned from a victim to a survivor, showcasing her resilience and empowerment.

The shadows cast by Complex PTSD are long and often invisible to the outside world, deeply affecting those who have endured prolonged abuse. This chapter has explored the profound effects of Complex PTSD, highlighting symptoms such as chronic emotional dysregulation, feelings of worthlessness, and constant hypervigilance. Understanding the impact of repeated trauma on both the mind and body is critical for survivors and those supporting them.

Personal narratives like Kelly's offer a glimpse into the daily struggles faced by survivors, who often grapple with dissociation, flashbacks, and emotional numbness. Kelly's story, in particular, emphasized the challenge of reconnecting with reality after enduring years of manipulation. It also underscores the importance of self-compassion, patience, and professional support in the recovery process.

Dr. Judith Herman stresses that recovery requires a comprehensive approach, including trauma-informed therapy, the creation of safe environments, and fostering supportive relationships. Recognizing that healing is not a linear process, but rather a series of advances and setbacks, is essential to maintaining hope and perseverance as survivors work toward reclaiming their lives.

Chapter 6:
Practical Approaches to Healing and Recovery

Recovering from narcissistic abuse is a complex journey that involves both practical strategies and emotional strength. In this chapter, we will discuss various methods that support the healing process, focusing on boosting self-esteem, creating healthy boundaries, and building strong, supportive relationships. From therapeutic techniques to self-care practices, these approaches are meant to help individuals reclaim their lives and achieve long-term emotional well-being. With expert insights and real-life stories, this chapter offers readers the tools and confidence they need to move forward on their path to recovery.

Step 1: Recognizing the Abuse

Self-Awareness: Validating Your Feelings and Experiences

The first step in healing from narcissistic abuse is self-awareness—acknowledging and accepting the reality of your experiences and emotions. Survivors often need to affirm the truth of their personal experiences, especially after prolonged manipulation. This section provides guidance and practical exercises that help individuals reconnect with their inner truth, such as journaling incidents of abuse and reflecting on the emotions they evoke. By validating their feelings and memories, survivors can begin to break down the self-doubt caused by the abuser. Through expert advice and engaging narratives, this section encourages readers to reclaim their story and build a solid foundation for healing.

Understanding Narcissistic Abuse: Recognizing It's Not Your Fault

Another crucial part of recovery is gaining a clear understanding of narcissistic abuse and its psychological effects. By learning about how this type of abuse works—beginning with subtle signs and leading to long-term emotional damage—survivors can recognize that they are not to blame for the harm done to them. Expert insights and educational resources offer clear explanations to dispel the confusion and self-doubt often caused by abusers. This understanding empowers survivors to begin the important work of psychological healing and to take back control of their personal narratives. It's a powerful step that helps individuals untangle the complex emotions and misconceptions left in the aftermath of abusive relationships.

Step 2 - Moving Forward by Letting Go of the Relationship

Cutting Ties with the Narcissist: A Crucial Step for Your Well-Being

Breaking off contact with a narcissist is an essential, though often difficult, part of the recovery process. This section outlines effective strategies for ending all forms of communication, highlighting the importance of both physical and digital separation. Techniques such as blocking phone numbers and social media accounts are vital to prevent unwanted interactions.

Managing mutual acquaintances and shared responsibilities is another challenge. Setting clear boundaries with mutual contacts about what information can be shared helps maintain privacy during this vulnerable time. In situations involving co-parenting or other shared responsibilities, establishing formal communication protocols through legal or mediation services can ensure that necessary interactions remain professional and impersonal. Using written communication for clarity and record-keeping can further protect against potential conflicts. These strategies help survivors maintain necessary connections while safeguarding their personal well-being and autonomy.

Facing the Backlash After Cutting Ties

When severing ties with a narcissist, backlash is common, including smear campaigns aimed at discrediting and isolating the survivor. Maya, a survivor, faced a smear campaign that spread false accusations throughout her social and professional circles. Legal expert Dr. Helena Swanson advises documenting every interaction and seeking legal advice if false claims threaten your reputation or safety. By strengthening her support network and consulting a lawyer, Maya was able to protect her professional integrity.

This section emphasizes avoiding direct confrontation with provocations while reinforcing support systems and utilizing legal resources when necessary. This approach helps survivors navigate the aftermath with strength, protecting their well-being from further harm.

Allowing Yourself to Grieve the Relationship

Grieving the end of a relationship, especially one marked by narcissistic abuse, is an important part of recovery. It's essential to recognize and allow feelings of denial, anger, bargaining, depression, and acceptance as valid stages of the grieving process. Engaging in therapy, journaling, or physical activities can provide outlets for processing these emotions. Dr. Karen Phelps, a grief counselor, stresses the importance of embracing grief without judgment and creating a safe space for healing, whether through support groups or personal reflection. By acknowledging grief as a necessary step, individuals can gradually move toward emotional clarity and recovery.

Step 3: Seeking Professional Support

Therapy Options

Recovering from narcissistic abuse often requires professional support, and understanding the different types of therapy is crucial for choosing the right path.

1. **Individual Therapy:**
2. Several forms of individual therapy are particularly effective for survivors of abuse.
    - **Cognitive-Behavioral Therapy (CBT)** helps individuals recognize and reframe negative thought patterns, reducing self-blame and irrational fears ingrained by the abuser.
    - **Dialectical Behavior Therapy (DBT)** focuses on developing emotional regulation and coping strategies to manage stress and emotional distress.

- ○ **Trauma-Informed Therapy** provides a holistic approach to recovery, addressing the full scope of trauma's impact on the mind and body. It offers a compassionate and sensitive framework, ensuring that the unique needs of survivors are met with comprehensive care.
3. **Group Therapy:**
4. Group therapy offers survivors the opportunity to connect with others who have experienced similar abuse. In this communal setting, individuals can share their stories, gain new perspectives, and feel supported in their recovery journey. The collective empathy and understanding fostered in group therapy help combat feelings of isolation, reinforcing the healing process through shared experiences and encouragement.

Choosing the Right Therapist

Finding a therapist with experience in trauma and abuse is critical for effective recovery. When searching for a therapist, it is important to ensure they have specialized training in handling trauma and abuse cases. This expertise ensures they can provide the understanding and tools necessary to help survivors navigate the complexities of their healing journey.

Selecting the Right Therapist for Trauma and Narcissistic Abuse Recovery

Finding a therapist specifically trained in trauma and familiar with the complexities of narcissistic abuse is essential for effective healing. Survivors are encouraged to seek out licensed professionals who specialize in trauma therapy by consulting directories and trusted mental health organizations. These resources offer valuable lists of qualified therapists, complete with credentials and areas of expertise, helping survivors locate a therapist whose experience aligns with their unique needs.

Key Questions to Ask a Potential Therapist

To ensure a therapist is well-equipped to address narcissistic abuse, it's important to ask targeted questions during the initial consultation. These may include:

- What specific training do you have in trauma therapy?
- Can you share examples of your experience working with survivors of narcissistic abuse?
- What therapeutic approaches do you use to address trauma from narcissistic relationships?

These questions help assess the therapist's familiarity with the dynamics of narcissistic abuse, ensuring that their approach aligns with the survivor's needs for effective recovery.

Step 4: Building a Support System

Support Groups: Joining Communities for Narcissistic Abuse Survivors

Engaging with support groups specifically designed for survivors of narcissistic abuse offers a vital space for healing. These groups provide emotional strength through shared experiences, allowing survivors to connect with others who have endured similar challenges. In these safe spaces, individuals can exchange personal stories, gain practical strategies for recovery, and receive encouragement. The collective experience of group support is a powerful tool for fostering resilience and rebuilding after abuse.

Leveraging Online Forums and Local Community Resources

Expanding support beyond formal groups, survivors can benefit from engaging with online forums and local resources. Online platforms provide 24/7 access to global communities of survivors, offering continuous support, shared advice, and a wealth of resources. Local community centers often host workshops, seminars, and healing activities that facilitate education and personal growth. By participating in both virtual and local communities, survivors can gain a broader understanding of narcissistic abuse and access diverse recovery tools.

Family and Friends: Educating Loved Ones About Narcissistic Abuse

Communicating openly with friends and family about the experience of narcissistic abuse is crucial for building a supportive network. Explaining the nature of the abuse and how it has impacted you helps loved ones understand your needs and offer appropriate support. Setting boundaries and managing expectations with friends and family ensures that their help aligns with your healing process. This informed support system can significantly reduce feelings of isolation and provide a reliable source of emotional and practical assistance, reinforcing resilience throughout recovery.

Step 5: Cultivating Self-Awareness and Mindfulness

Mindfulness Practices: Introducing Techniques to Reduce Anxiety and Stay Grounded

In the recovery from narcissistic abuse, developing mindfulness is a crucial component of emotional healing. This section introduces simple but effective practices such as meditation, breathing exercises, and mindful walking, each chosen to reduce anxiety and increase present-moment awareness. These techniques are designed to help survivors calm their minds, focus their thoughts, and regain emotional balance. Real-life examples and expert insights illustrate how these practices can significantly improve mental clarity and emotional stability, providing survivors with practical tools to regain control over their emotional responses.

Journaling: A Tool for Emotional Processing and Progress Tracking

Journaling offers a private and therapeutic outlet for expressing the complex emotions that survivors may struggle to verbalize. It provides a safe space for documenting thoughts, feelings, and experiences regularly, helping individuals process their emotions and track their progress over time. By reflecting on written entries, survivors can identify patterns in their emotional responses, gaining valuable insights into their healing journey. Experts highlight how journaling fosters a deep connection with one's inner self, contributing to emotional clarity and resilience throughout recovery.

Self-Reflection Exercises: Identifying Triggers and Healing Needs

Self-reflection is a key part of building self-awareness, particularly for those recovering from psychological abuse. Techniques such as daily reflection prompts, emotional inventories, and guided reflections are useful tools for understanding emotional triggers and personal healing needs. These exercises encourage individuals to explore their emotional landscape, helping them recognize and manage the specific triggers that may disrupt their recovery. By enhancing self-awareness, survivors can adopt a more mindful and controlled approach to healing, ensuring steady progress.

Step 6: Reclaiming Your Identity

Rediscovering Personal Values and Interests

Narcissistic abuse often overshadows a survivor's personal values, interests, and goals, making it essential to reconnect with their true selves as part of the healing process. This section offers techniques to help individuals differentiate between genuine personal interests and those imposed by their abuser. Through reflective exercises such as journaling and guided meditation, survivors can rediscover their core values and set new, meaningful personal goals.

One helpful exercise involves listing hobbies or activities enjoyed before the abusive relationship and reflecting on why they brought joy. Another technique is to envision an ideal day free from external influences, revealing hidden passions and aspirations. For instance, Alicia rekindled her love for painting, which she had neglected during her marriage. Through therapy and support groups, she returned to her art and even hosted a small exhibition, a milestone that boosted her self-esteem and grounded her recovery process.

Dr. Lisa Firestone, a clinical psychologist, explains, "Reconnecting with one's true values and interests is crucial for rebuilding a sense of self and autonomy." This process is about reclaiming what was lost while fostering a more authentic, fulfilling life. By setting new personal goals, survivors can create a path forward aligned with their true selves—whether through a new career, volunteering, or learning a new skill.

Promoting Independence Through Engaging Activities

Restoring independence and self-efficacy is key to reclaiming identity after abuse. This section highlights activities such as solo travel, exploring new hobbies, and participating in community service, which empower survivors to regain confidence and autonomy. These pursuits are more than just hobbies—they are fundamental to rebuilding self-esteem and agency.

Inspiring stories of individuals who have transformed their self-perception through independent activities emphasize how such endeavors can be life-changing. Engaging in new challenges can shift a survivor's self-image, fostering a renewed sense of joy and purpose. Expert discussions reinforce that these activities are pivotal tools for emotional resilience and empowerment, essential for anyone on the journey to recovery.

Navigating the path to healing and recovery from narcissistic abuse requires a holistic approach, integrating self-awareness, self-care, and continuous support. This chapter has outlined a clear step-by-step guide to essential strategies for recovery, with a focus on acknowledging and addressing the profound effects of abuse.

A key element in this process is understanding the manipulative tactics, such as gaslighting and emotional control, used by narcissists. Recognizing and labeling these behaviors allows survivors to dismantle the distorted narratives imposed by their abusers and reclaim their self-worth.

Practical tools like daily affirmations, journaling, and creative expression are crucial for reinforcing self-esteem and nurturing self-compassion. These activities help survivors reconnect with their true selves, fostering a sense of empowerment and personal growth.

Support systems are equally vital. Whether through therapy, support groups, or online forums, connecting with others who validate and understand one's experiences offers critical emotional and psychological backing. Expert perspectives underline the importance of these networks in encouraging sustained healing and growth.

Finally, acknowledging personal progress—even in small increments—helps maintain motivation and celebrate recovery milestones. Setting realistic goals and practicing mindfulness are important for managing setbacks and ensuring long-term improvement. As survivors adapt these recovery strategies to their evolving needs, they can continue to grow, heal, and thrive.

Chapter 7:
Establishing Boundaries and Nurturing Self-Love

Establishing healthy boundaries and fostering self-love are critical steps in rebuilding your life after narcissistic abuse. This chapter offers practical advice on how to set and maintain boundaries to protect your emotional well-being and nurture respectful relationships. Additionally, it explores techniques for cultivating self-love, such as daily affirmations, journaling, and creative outlets like art and travel. Through expert insights and real-life stories, readers will discover how to protect their emotional health, build self-esteem, and develop a deep, compassionate relationship with themselves.

Practical Advice on Setting Healthy Boundaries with Real-Life Examples

Setting healthy boundaries is essential for preserving personal well-being and ensuring relationships remain respectful. This section provides actionable steps on defining and communicating your limits clearly and assertively. For instance, setting specific times to address work interruptions helps create clear expectations. Experts emphasize the importance of consistently communicating these boundaries—stating them clearly, adjusting as needed, and ensuring they are respected. This approach helps individuals effectively assert their needs and fosters environments where personal space and preferences are honored.

Boundaries protect emotional energy, maintain self-esteem, and allow individuals to disengage from toxic or over-demanding relationships. Recognizing and respecting personal limits helps prevent burnout and emotional distress, making boundary-setting a crucial skill in both personal and professional contexts. This section also explores the different types of boundaries—emotional, physical, intellectual, and spiritual—and how establishing these limits helps maintain a balanced lifestyle. For example, limiting time spent on social media can improve mental health, while setting personal boundaries in relationships can prevent overcommitment. Each boundary should align with your values and priorities, reinforcing your sense of self and enhancing your interactions with others.

Examples of Setting Boundaries in Various Situations

Setting and enforcing boundaries, particularly after experiencing abuse, involves recognizing your own limits, clearly communicating them to others, and maintaining consistency in upholding them. Below are practical examples of how to set boundaries in different areas of life:

1. **In Personal Relationships:**
   Example: "I need time to unwind after work. Let's talk later in the evening." This sets a clear boundary for personal space.
2. **At the Workplace:**
   Example: "I prefer to keep personal matters separate from work. Let's keep the conversation professional." This ensures that boundaries are respected in a work environment.
3. **With Family:**
   Example: "I won't be answering calls during meals." This boundary prioritizes personal or family time without interruptions.
4. **In Social Settings:**
   Example: "I'm not comfortable with last-minute plans. Please give me a heads up next time." This establishes the need for respect regarding social commitments.

Maintaining boundaries can be challenging, especially when others test or disregard them. However, consistency is key to ensuring that boundaries continue to protect and respect your well-being.

Strategies for Upholding Boundaries

This section outlines effective strategies for consistently upholding boundaries:

1. **Assertiveness Training:**
   Learning to express your needs confidently, without aggression, is essential. For instance, saying, "I appreciate

your interest, but I'm not comfortable discussing this," reinforces personal limits in a respectful way.
2. **Support Networks:**
Relying on friends, family, or support groups who understand and respect your boundaries can strengthen your efforts. Sharing experiences within these groups can provide reassurance and encouragement to maintain your boundaries.
3. **Regular Self-Reflection:**
Periodically reviewing your boundaries helps ensure they are still serving their intended purpose. Asking yourself, "Are my boundaries working for me? Do I feel respected?" keeps you aligned with your needs and promotes ongoing boundary maintenance.

By using these techniques, the importance of boundary-setting for long-term mental health and relationship management is emphasized. Real-world examples are provided throughout to show the positive impact of maintaining consistent boundaries.

Techniques for Cultivating Self-Love and Self-Compassion

Developing self-love and self-compassion is crucial for emotional well-being, particularly after experiencing narcissistic abuse. This guide outlines several practices that help individuals nurture a positive self-image and build emotional resilience. **Daily affirmations** are a simple yet effective method to reinforce self-worth and combat negative thinking. Reciting positive statements each morning, such as "I am deserving of happiness," can significantly shift one's mindset toward optimism.

Additionally, **journaling** offers a reflective outlet for processing emotions, enabling a deeper understanding of personal experiences and promoting mental clarity. Through the practice of writing, individuals can explore complex feelings and track their progress, gaining insights into their healing journey.

Beyond these reflective practices, engaging in **creative expression** through art or travel can open new avenues for self-discovery and joy. Whether through painting, writing, or playing music, creative activities offer a therapeutic way to express emotions and thoughts without judgment. Similarly, travel broadens horizons and provides new insights into oneself and the world, fostering personal growth and self-appreciation.

These activities, whether introspective or exploratory, support a journey of self-discovery and greater self-acceptance. They help individuals connect with their inner selves, boost self-esteem, and foster a resilient mindset, ultimately benefiting all areas of life.

Daily Affirmations and Journaling

Incorporating daily affirmations into your routine can be transformative, helping to shift your mindset and elevate self-esteem. Repeating affirmations such as "I am worthy of good things" or "I choose kindness toward myself" encourages positive mental dialogue, replacing negative thoughts with affirmations of self-worth.

When paired with journaling, the process becomes even more powerful. Journaling allows individuals to reflect on their emotions, track their progress, and gain insights into their personal growth. It provides a private, structured space to explore complex feelings, which enhances emotional awareness and processing. This combination of affirmations and journaling creates a strong foundation for a positive self-image and emotional resilience.

Sample Affirmations to Begin With:

1. "I deserve love and respect from others and myself."
2. "I am worthy of happiness and peace."
3. "Every day, I grow stronger and more resilient."
4. "I trust my intuition and honor my needs."
5. "I release my past and live fully in the present."

Now, take a moment to reflect on what you need to hear most. What words would lift your spirits? Write them down and incorporate them into your daily routine. This practice is a powerful step toward reclaiming your self-esteem and joy.

Journal Prompts for Reflection and Healing

Here are some thoughtful journal prompts to facilitate reflection and emotional healing. Use them to explore your feelings, experiences, and growth:

1. **Identify and Reflect:** What are three emotions you frequently felt during the relationship? Describe situations where these emotions were most intense.
2. **Understanding Manipulation:** Reflect on a time you felt manipulated. What were the signs? How can recognizing these signs help you in the future?
3. **Reclaiming Self:** Write about the things you loved doing before the relationship that you stopped doing during it. How can you start reintegrating these activities into your life?
4. **Self-Compassion:** What would you tell a friend who went through similar experiences? Try to extend the same compassion to yourself.
5. **Future Boundaries:** What boundaries do you wish you had set in your past relationship? How can you ensure these boundaries are respected in future relationships?
6. **Celebrating Growth:** What are some strengths you have discovered about yourself since leaving the abusive situation?
7. **Visions of the Future:** Where do you see yourself in one year? What steps can you take to get there?

By regularly engaging with these affirmations and journal prompts, you'll deepen your connection to your inner self, fostering self-love, resilience, and emotional growth.

Creative Expression Through Art and Travel

Engaging in creative activities like painting, writing, or playing music can be incredibly therapeutic and enriching. These forms of artistic expression provide a way to release emotions constructively, offering individuals an outlet to process their feelings. Creating art allows one to visualize and confront emotional issues that may be difficult to express verbally. This therapeutic approach not only fosters emotional healing but also offers a fulfilling, creative escape.

Similarly, travel serves as a powerful tool for self-discovery and personal growth. Immersing yourself in new cultures and environments expands your perspective and deepens your understanding of the world. Experiencing different ways of life fosters a stronger connection with others, promoting a sense of empathy and appreciation for diversity. Additionally, the challenges encountered while traveling strengthen adaptability and resilience, offering valuable life lessons and personal insights.

Both creative expression and travel are vital in nurturing self-compassion and enhancing mental well-being. These activities encourage exploration of one's inner thoughts and feelings, free from judgment, fostering a sense of freedom and self-acceptance. Through these endeavors, individuals can discover new passions, reconnect with their authentic selves, and experience a renewed sense of purpose. Creative expression and exploration contribute significantly to building a more fulfilling and enriched life.

The Importance of Self-Care Routines and How to Establish Them

Why Self-Care is Essential

Self-care routines are key to maintaining mental, emotional, and physical health. Far from being indulgent, self-care is a necessary practice that brings stability and relief from daily stress. Regular self-care can improve mood, reduce anxiety, and enhance productivity. Research from the American Psychological Association highlights that consistent self-care can lower stress levels and prevent burnout. According to Dr. Kristen Neff, a leading researcher in self-compassion, "Self-care allows us to recharge, fostering resilience and emotional well-being."

Steps to Establish a Self-Care Routine

1. **Identify Your Needs:**
   Reflect on areas of your life that need more attention—whether mental, physical, or emotional. Understanding where you're feeling drained helps tailor a self-care plan to your specific needs.
2. **Set Realistic Goals:**
   Start with small, achievable goals that fit into your daily routine. For example, aim for five minutes of morning meditation or take a short walk during lunch breaks.
3. **Incorporate Variety:**
   A well-rounded self-care routine includes activities that address different aspects of well-being. This could include

physical exercise, mindfulness practices, creative hobbies, or spending time with loved ones.
4. **Schedule It In:**
Treat self-care like a non-negotiable appointment. Whether it's a yoga class, journaling, or a relaxing bath, scheduling these activities ensures they become a regular part of your life.
5. **Reflect and Adjust:**
Periodically assess whether your self-care routine is effective. If certain activities aren't providing the relief you need, adjust them and try something new.

Anecdotal Evidence

Take Ashley, a corporate executive on the verge of burnout. By incorporating self-care practices like morning meditation, weekly art classes, and regular nature walks, she regained focus and reduced stress. This newfound balance improved her work performance and deepened her connection to herself and her loved ones.

Expert Insights

Dr. Neff emphasizes the role of self-compassion in self-care, explaining, "It's about treating yourself with the same kindness and care that you would offer a friend." This shift in perspective transforms self-care from another task on a to-do list into an act of self-love.

Practical Examples of Self-Care Routines

1. **Morning Routine:**
Start your day with mindfulness by meditating or practicing deep breathing. Follow up with a healthy breakfast and light exercise to set a positive tone for the day.
2. **Midday Breaks:**
Use your lunch break to decompress—take a walk, read a book, or engage in a hobby that brings you joy.
3. **Evening Wind-Down:**
End your day with relaxing activities like journaling, taking a warm bath, or practicing gentle yoga.

Long-Term Benefits

Regular self-care leads to lasting improvements in both mental and physical health. It helps build resilience, enabling you to handle life's challenges with greater ease. Investing in self-care creates a foundation of well-being that supports every aspect of life, leading to greater balance and overall satisfaction.

Conclusion

This chapter has offered practical strategies for establishing healthy boundaries and nurturing self-compassion and self-respect. Boundaries are vital for protecting emotional well-being and fostering respectful relationships. By reflecting on journal prompts like:

- "What are my non-negotiables in relationships?"
- "When do I feel most uncomfortable, and what boundary could help?"
- "How can I communicate my needs clearly and assertively?"

You can identify areas where boundaries are needed. Setting clear limits, stating your needs, and practicing saying no without guilt are key steps in maintaining personal space and emotional health.

Cultivating self-love involves integrating daily affirmations like "I am worthy of love and respect" into your routine and using journaling exercises to reflect on your positive attributes and accomplishments. Engaging in creative activities such as painting, writing, or traveling helps with self-expression and allows for reconnection with your authentic self.

Establishing a consistent self-care routine is essential for achieving balance and long-term well-being. By recognizing your needs, setting achievable goals, diversifying self-care activities, and regularly reflecting on their effectiveness, you create a sustainable self-care practice. Remember, self-care is not an indulgence, but a necessity for leading a fulfilling and healthy life.

Chapter 8:
Building Healthy Relationships

Creating and sustaining healthy relationships is essential for living a balanced and fulfilling life. Whether in romantic, familial, or platonic relationships, understanding the key characteristics of positive interactions can greatly improve emotional well-being. This chapter delves into the core elements of healthy relationships, such as mutual respect, clear communication, and emotional support. It offers practical advice for identifying warning signs, fostering trust, and developing intimacy. Through expert guidance and real-life examples, readers will gain valuable tools to form and maintain meaningful, supportive relationships that contribute to long-term happiness and stability.

Defining a Healthy Relationship: Key Characteristics and Foundations

Healthy relationships, whether family ties, friendships, or romantic partnerships, are built on essential qualities like mutual respect, trust, and open communication. These core traits serve different roles depending on the relationship type. In family relationships, they strengthen bonds through unconditional support and acceptance; in friendships, they create a safe space for personal growth and sharing; and in romantic relationships, they foster deep connections that can withstand life's challenges.

Example of Healthy Family Dynamics:

In the Walker family, open communication is key. Every Sunday, they hold a "no-judgment" meeting where everyone, including the children, shares their week's highlights and challenges. This practice has strengthened mutual respect and understanding, allowing the family to support one another through various life events.

Example of a Healthy Friendship:

Leah and Rachel's long-standing friendship thrives on active listening and constructive feedback. When Rachel was struggling with a tough career decision, Leah offered emotional support and thoughtful advice without judgment, helping Rachel make an informed decision.

Example of a Healthy Romantic Relationship:

Maria and Charlie exemplify a strong romantic relationship. From the start, they established a routine of weekly discussions to address concerns and express appreciation. This habit deepened their trust and mutual respect. When Charlie faced job loss, their foundation of open communication helped them navigate the stress, reinforcing their bond rather than weakening it.

Relationship experts, like Dr. Elaine Foster, emphasize that these foundational traits—respect, trust, and communication—are crucial for nurturing healthy connections. These qualities not only promote individual well-being but also enhance the resilience of relationships, allowing them to thrive even through difficult times.

Recognizing Red Flags in Relationships

This section highlights common warning signs that suggest potential problems in relationships. Spotting these red flags early is critical for safeguarding emotional health and cultivating more respectful, supportive connections. Red flags can manifest as poor communication, disrespect, or controlling behavior.

Communication Issues:

One partner might consistently avoid discussing feelings or relationship challenges, leaving issues unresolved and creating emotional distance.

Disrespect:
Frequent interruptions, dismissive comments, or mocking behaviors can undermine mutual respect, leading to diminished self-esteem over time.

Controlling Behaviors:

Control might involve dictating a partner's choices regarding their appearance, social interactions, or activities. Dr. Lisa Orban, a clinical psychologist specializing in relationships, warns, "Controlling behavior can isolate individuals from their support systems and erode their autonomy, leading to unhealthy relationship dynamics."

Anecdote for a Romantic Relationship:

Kim and Mike's relationship began with excitement, but Kim soon noticed Mike making decisions for both of them without her input, especially regarding her clothing and social circle. Initially dismissing it as care, she realized it was controlling when Mike became upset if she acted independently. This gradual shift left Kim feeling stifled and controlled.

Anecdote for a Friendship:

Kelsy and Kara had been close friends since college, but Kara's behavior changed when Kelsy entered a new relationship. Kara began demanding excessive time and became upset when Kelsy made plans that didn't include her. This strain in their friendship demonstrates how controlling behaviors can affect even platonic relationships.

The impact of these behaviors is significant. Poor communication can result in a lack of empathy and understanding, while disrespect can cause emotional harm and undermine trust. Controlling behaviors shift the power dynamics in relationships, leading to dependency and an environment of fear.

Forming healthy relationships, whether in family, friendships, or romantic partnerships, is essential for emotional well-being and long-term happiness. By focusing on mutual respect, open communication, and trust, individuals can cultivate supportive, resilient connections. Recognizing and addressing red flags early on is vital to protecting emotional health and ensuring that relationships remain respectful and balanced.

Rebuilding Trust and Intimacy After Abuse

Rebuilding trust and fostering intimacy after experiencing abuse can feel overwhelming, but it is entirely achievable with the right mindset and support system. In this section, we share the stories of individuals who have successfully navigated this challenging journey, offering real-life examples of how they restored trust and rebuilt meaningful relationships.

One story features Anthony, who endured emotional abuse from a sibling, including gaslighting and belittling. Through therapy and support groups, Anthony learned to set boundaries and slowly built trust with new friends who respected his space and offered empathy without judgment. His friends gave him the time he needed to open up and made sure their interactions were supportive rather than overwhelming. They frequently checked in on his well-being without pressing for more details than he was comfortable sharing. Anthony's journey highlights the importance of surrounding yourself with patient, supportive individuals who respect your healing process.

Another example involves Kendrick, who survived an abusive romantic relationship and initially struggled with trusting others. He found solace in writing and connecting with people who shared similar experiences. Over time, Kendrick communicated his fears and expectations clearly in relationships, helping him build a new, healthy relationship based on mutual respect and understanding.

Psychologists like Dr. Nina Jackson, an expert in trauma recovery, offer insights into rebuilding trust. Dr. Jackson explains, "Trust begins with oneself. Survivors must first develop a trusting relationship with their inner selves through self-compassion and acknowledgment of their resilience." She recommends setting small, manageable trust goals in relationships and regularly reflecting on one's comfort levels, ensuring open communication with partners.

Rebuilding trust and intimacy is not only possible but can lead to deeply rewarding relationships. These stories serve as a reminder that, with time, patience, and the right strategies, survivors can find healthy, loving relationships.

Conclusion

Forming healthy relationships is a crucial step in recovering from narcissistic abuse. This chapter has explored what constitutes a healthy relationship, provided tools for recognizing red flags, and offered strategies for rebuilding trust and intimacy post-abuse.

Healthy relationships are built on mutual respect, trust, open communication, and emotional support. Stories like Maria and Charlie's illustrate how addressing unhealthy patterns can lead to relationships grounded in trust and respect. Recognizing red flags early—such as poor communication, disrespect, and controlling behavior—helps prevent emotional harm. For instance, a friend who constantly belittles your achievements or a partner who dictates your interactions with others are clear signs of a toxic relationship.

Rebuilding trust and intimacy after abuse requires patience and small, gradual steps. Survivors like Anthony, who learned to set boundaries and communicate effectively, show that it's possible to develop loving, supportive relationships after abuse. Expert advice stresses the importance of self-awareness, setting realistic expectations, and creating a secure foundation for future relationships.

Chapter 9:
Moving Forward

The journey of healing from narcissistic abuse is filled with both victories and challenges. Moving forward goes beyond just recovery—it's about rediscovering yourself and building a future grounded in resilience and joy. This chapter offers insights on maintaining progress, handling setbacks, and evolving continuously. It underscores the importance of self-awareness, setting achievable goals, and celebrating personal growth. Readers will be equipped with the tools and inspiration to navigate their path toward a brighter, more empowered future.

Sustaining Progress and Managing Setbacks

Recovery from narcissistic abuse requires ongoing dedication to personal growth and the resilience to face setbacks. This section provides strategies for maintaining progress while managing challenges along the way.

Bella's story exemplifies these challenges. After making significant progress in her recovery, Bella had a relapse when she unexpectedly encountered her abuser at a social gathering. This encounter brought back feelings of insecurity and self-doubt. However, Bella used **mindfulness**—the practice of staying present without judgment—to regain control of her emotions. By reconnecting with her support network, revisiting therapy, and reaffirming her recovery goals, Bella was able to regain her sense of balance.

Mindfulness techniques like deep breathing, guided imagery, and meditation are invaluable tools for maintaining emotional stability. Dr. Amy Patel advises incorporating mindfulness into daily routines to manage stress and enhance self-awareness.

Setting **realistic goals** is another crucial part of recovery. These goals might include creating healthy boundaries in relationships, attending regular therapy sessions, or committing to daily self-care practices. Keeping track of these goals can be made easier through journaling, using apps, or joining accountability groups for support.

Celebrating small achievements is vital for boosting self-esteem and motivation. Acknowledging even minor successes, such as managing anxiety for a day or sticking to self-care routines, reinforces positive progress. Simple rewards, like indulging in a favorite activity or sharing accomplishments with a supportive friend, help sustain long-term recovery.

Redefining Your Identity and Future

After breaking free from a narcissistic relationship, many individuals embark on a journey of rediscovering their identity and envisioning a future aligned with their true selves. This section highlights how survivors can reclaim parts of themselves that were overshadowed by manipulation and control.

Clara's story is a powerful example of this transformation. After leaving a controlling partner, she rediscovered her passion for painting—a hobby she had abandoned during her relationship. Reconnecting with this creative outlet helped Clara rediscover her authentic self and marked a key step in her recovery journey.

Jessie's story offers another inspiring example. After separating from an abusive partner, Jessie chose to leave his high-stress finance job to pursue a career in teaching, a field that better aligned with his values of helping others. This career shift not only represented a professional change but also symbolized Jessie's commitment to living a life that reflected his core beliefs and aspirations.

Both stories illustrate that moving forward after abuse often involves reclaiming passions and values that were stifled during unhealthy relationships. By doing so, survivors not only heal but also build futures that are true to their desires, fostering a sense of fulfillment and empowerment.

Continuing Education and Resources for Lifelong Resilience

The journey of recovery from narcissistic abuse is greatly supported by continued education and access to helpful resources. This section provides a curated guide to tools and educational materials that empower survivors to build a resilient and fulfilling life. Key recommendations include influential books such as *It's Not You* by Dr. Ramani Durvasula and *How to Do the Work: Recognize Your Patterns, Heal from Your Past, and Create Your Self* by Nicole LePera. Additionally, workshops offered by organizations like the National Domestic Violence Hotline are highlighted as valuable resources.

Support groups and online courses also play an essential role in this ongoing process. These resources often focus on understanding narcissistic relationship dynamics, developing emotional intelligence, and strengthening communication skills. Platforms like Udemy and Coursera offer courses on these topics, taught by qualified professionals, which also provide peer support and engagement.

Experts emphasize the importance of lifelong learning and the power of community support in maintaining long-term resilience and well-being. Regular engagement with these resources not only reinforces the recovery strategies discussed throughout this book but also equips survivors with the tools to thrive in their post-abuse lives, empowering them to face future challenges with strength and confidence.

Conclusion

This chapter offers survivors practical guidance to explore new interests and establish goals aligned with their personal values, helping foster a renewed sense of autonomy and self-worth. Techniques like mindfulness exercises, journaling to discover hidden passions, and setting small, achievable goals are discussed to support the gradual creation of a new, authentic life after abuse.

By embracing these new paths and celebrating every small victory, survivors can significantly enhance their self-esteem and independence, setting the stage for a future filled with fulfillment and empowerment.

Chapter 10:
Embracing Empowerment and Self-Advocacy

The final phase in the journey of healing from narcissistic abuse is centered on empowerment and the ability to advocate for oneself. This chapter focuses on cultivating a mindset of empowerment, developing self-advocacy skills, and creating a life where survivors not only recover but also thrive. By embracing these key principles, survivors can fully reclaim their autonomy and rebuild their lives with confidence and purpose.

The Power of Self-Advocacy

Self-advocacy is a critical skill for anyone recovering from narcissistic abuse. Learning to assert your needs, speak up for your rights, and establish healthy boundaries empowers survivors to regain control over their lives. Often, those who have endured abuse are conditioned to suppress their voices, feeling hesitant to express their needs or desires. This chapter stresses the importance of unlearning that conditioning and embracing self-advocacy as a means to reclaim one's power.

What is Self-Advocacy?
At its core, self-advocacy is about clearly communicating your needs and boundaries without fear of rejection or retaliation. This doesn't mean being aggressive, but rather being assertive, ensuring that your voice is heard and respected. Advocacy is about standing up for your emotional and physical well-being and expecting the same level of respect you afford to others.

Why is it Essential?
Self-advocacy is crucial in all areas of life—whether it's standing firm in personal relationships, negotiating boundaries in the workplace, or seeking appropriate care in healthcare settings. By developing self-advocacy skills, survivors can protect themselves from further

harm and create environments that promote their mental, emotional, and physical well-being.

Steps to Developing Self-Advocacy Skills:

1. **Know Your Rights:** Understanding that you have the right to express your needs, feelings, and boundaries is foundational. Survivors must recognize that their voice is important and deserves to be heard.
2. **Practice Assertive Communication:** Learning how to communicate in a clear, respectful, and firm manner is key. Assertiveness training, role-playing, or even journaling scenarios where you assert your needs can be beneficial.
3. **Seek Support:** Engage with a mentor, therapist, or support group to reinforce the importance of self-advocacy. These communities can provide validation and encouragement as you practice standing up for yourself.
4. **Start Small:** Begin with manageable steps. Advocate for yourself in low-stakes situations, such as expressing a preference in a conversation or setting a small boundary. Gradually, this skill will grow, and you will feel more confident asserting yourself in larger areas of life.

Reclaiming Autonomy Through Empowerment

Empowerment means more than just surviving—it's about thriving. Moving from victimhood to empowerment is an essential shift that allows survivors to take charge of their lives again. This chapter focuses on ways to foster this sense of empowerment.

Building Resilience:
Resilience is the ability to bounce back from adversity, and developing it is crucial for survivors of abuse. Resilience doesn't mean ignoring pain or never feeling vulnerable—it means being able to face challenges, process them, and come out stronger. Through resilience, survivors can learn to handle life's ups and downs with a sense of purpose and strength.

Cultivating a Growth Mindset:
A growth mindset is the belief that abilities and intelligence can be developed over time. Embracing a growth mindset helps survivors of abuse view setbacks not as failures, but as opportunities for learning

and growth. This shift in perspective can be empowering, as it encourages individuals to seek out new challenges and continue evolving.

Creating a Vision for the Future

One of the most important elements of moving forward after abuse is creating a new vision for your life. After leaving a toxic relationship, many survivors feel lost, as their sense of identity may have been tied to their abuser. Rebuilding that identity involves looking forward and imagining a future where personal goals, values, and passions take center stage.

Setting Meaningful Goals:
Survivors should focus on setting goals that reflect their true desires and aspirations, rather than the expectations of others. These goals may involve career changes, educational pursuits, or personal growth, such as learning a new skill or developing a hobby. The key is to set goals that feel authentic and rewarding.

Finding Your Purpose:
Purpose gives life meaning and direction. After enduring abuse, reconnecting with a sense of purpose is vital for emotional healing. Whether it's through volunteer work, creative expression, or a new career path, finding ways to contribute to the world that align with personal values can foster a deep sense of fulfillment.

Celebrating Successes:
Every step forward should be celebrated. Whether it's overcoming a small hurdle or achieving a long-term goal, acknowledging progress reinforces a positive mindset. Celebrating these wins, no matter how small, helps to boost confidence and encourages continued growth.

The Role of Community in Sustained Empowerment

No one heals alone. Community plays a vital role in long-term recovery and empowerment. Support networks—whether through friends, family, therapy groups, or online forums—offer the validation, empathy, and encouragement necessary for survivors to continue thriving.

Building a Supportive Network:
Survivors need people around them who uplift, inspire, and validate their experiences. Cultivating relationships with people who respect boundaries and encourage personal growth is essential for sustained healing. Trusted friends, mentors, and support groups can help survivors remain focused on their recovery goals and provide emotional and mental support when challenges arise.

Giving Back to the Community:
Once survivors reach a place of stability and empowerment, many find it fulfilling to give back. Sharing experiences and helping others on their journey can be an incredibly empowering and healing act. Volunteering, mentoring, or simply offering a supportive ear to someone who is just beginning their recovery can strengthen one's sense of purpose and solidify the progress they've made.

Conclusion: Stepping Into Your Power

The journey from narcissistic abuse to empowerment is transformative. As you move forward, embracing self-advocacy, cultivating resilience, and fostering a growth mindset are crucial steps toward reclaiming your life. This chapter has provided strategies for standing up for yourself, building a future rooted in personal goals, and finding empowerment in community.

By integrating these tools into your daily life, you can continue to thrive, embrace your newfound autonomy, and confidently step into the future you deserve. Empowerment is a lifelong journey, and with each step, you grow stronger, more resilient, and more aligned with your authentic self.

Embracing Lifelong Learning and Self-Discovery

Empowerment is not a one-time achievement—it's a continuous process of learning, evolving, and discovering new layers of yourself. As survivors of narcissistic abuse move forward, it's essential to remain open to growth and curiosity. Lifelong learning, whether through formal education, self-exploration, or new experiences, fuels personal development and deepens self-awareness.

Pursuing New Skills and Knowledge:
Education, in its many forms, can be incredibly empowering.

Whether you're learning a new skill, pursuing a hobby, or deepening your understanding of a subject that sparks interest, embracing new knowledge can rebuild confidence and open new opportunities. This chapter encourages survivors to continue seeking out new experiences—whether it's through courses, workshops, or creative pursuits—that challenge and inspire them. Each new achievement not only enhances personal growth but also reinforces the sense of control over one's life.

Exploring Your Passions:
Narcissistic abuse often stifles personal interests, leaving survivors disconnected from their true passions. Reconnecting with these passions is an essential part of rediscovering oneself. Explore activities that bring joy, spark creativity, or foster relaxation. Whether it's painting, writing, gardening, or traveling, engaging in activities that align with your inner self helps rebuild self-worth and provides a sense of fulfillment. This exploration is not just a form of healing, but a celebration of autonomy and individuality.

Mindfulness and Reflection as Ongoing Practices:
Mindfulness continues to play a pivotal role in maintaining emotional balance and fostering personal growth. As survivors move further along their path to empowerment, integrating mindfulness into everyday routines can help manage stress, maintain self-awareness, and keep the focus on long-term healing. Regular reflection, through practices like journaling or meditation, encourages a deeper understanding of emotional triggers, personal strengths, and the areas in life that require nurturing.

Transforming Pain into Purpose: The Power of Personal Narrative

One of the most powerful aspects of recovery is the ability to transform past pain into a source of strength and purpose. Survivors of narcissistic abuse often find healing in redefining their narrative—not as victims, but as empowered individuals who have overcome significant challenges. This chapter explores how reshaping your personal story can provide closure, inspire others, and instill a renewed sense of purpose.

Sharing Your Story:
Telling your story, whether in private conversations, support groups,

or public platforms, can be deeply healing. By sharing experiences, survivors can process their trauma in a constructive way, gain validation, and help others who may be navigating similar paths. Many survivors also find that speaking out about their abuse empowers them to reclaim control over their narrative and assert their resilience in the face of adversity.

Helping Others on Their Journey:
Empowerment can be found in helping others who are still in the process of recovery. Offering guidance, sharing experiences, or volunteering with support organizations are powerful ways to transform the pain of the past into a positive force. By supporting others, survivors can continue to grow, gain perspective, and further solidify their own healing process.

Defining Success on Your Own Terms:
An essential part of moving forward is defining what success means to you—independent of societal expectations or past limitations imposed by others. Success, for survivors of abuse, isn't always about external achievements; it's often measured by internal milestones, such as feeling at peace, setting healthy boundaries, or rediscovering joy. This chapter encourages readers to define success in a way that feels authentic and fulfilling to them, allowing for personal growth without external pressures.

Final Thoughts: Stepping Into the Future with Confidence

As this chapter—and the book—comes to a close, it's important to recognize the incredible journey survivors have embarked on. The path from abuse to empowerment is challenging, but it is also filled with opportunities for growth, self-discovery, and transformation. By developing self-advocacy skills, embracing a mindset of lifelong learning, and finding purpose in both personal and communal contributions, survivors can continue to evolve and thrive.

Empowerment is not just about healing from the past—it's about building a future where you live authentically, with confidence and purpose. It's about acknowledging your resilience, celebrating your progress, and allowing yourself to dream without limitations. As you step into the next chapter of your life, remember that you are not defined by the abuse you endured, but by the strength, wisdom, and empowerment you've gained through your recovery.

This is your story, and you have the power to shape it. With the tools and insights shared throughout this book, you are equipped to create a life filled with resilience, joy, and fulfillment. Your journey of healing and empowerment is ongoing, and with each step forward, you reaffirm your strength, your value, and your ability to thrive.

Chapter 11:
Forging New Paths and Living Authentically

As the healing journey progresses, the focus shifts toward creating a life that is fully aligned with who you are, free from the shadows of narcissistic abuse. Chapter 12 delves into the art of living authentically, building on the foundations of self-empowerment and self-awareness. It offers guidance on how to create a future that reflects your true desires, values, and aspirations. In this chapter, readers will explore how to let go of the past, embrace new opportunities, and move forward with confidence and purpose.

Letting Go of the Past: Releasing the Hold of Abuse

One of the most critical steps in living authentically is learning how to release the past, especially the pain and trauma caused by narcissistic abuse. Letting go doesn't mean forgetting—it means freeing yourself from the emotional burden and allowing healing to take root.

Forgiveness as a Personal Journey:
Forgiving the abuser is often seen as a step toward closure, but it's important to recognize that forgiveness is a deeply personal choice. It's not about excusing the abuser's behavior but rather releasing the emotional hold that anger or resentment may have over your life. Forgiveness can also mean forgiving yourself for any perceived shortcomings or regrets about the past. By practicing self-compassion and focusing on your present, you give yourself permission to heal without carrying the weight of the past.

Healing Without Closure:
Sometimes, survivors do not receive the closure they desire from the abuser—no apology, no acknowledgment of wrongdoing. This can be painful, but it's essential to understand that closure doesn't have to come from external sources. You have the power to create your own closure by accepting the situation for what it is and choosing to focus on your own growth and healing.

Embracing New Opportunities: Redefining Your Life on Your Own Terms

With the past in perspective, the next step is to actively create a life that aligns with your values and dreams. This involves embracing new opportunities, rediscovering passions, and taking control of your future.

Redefining Success for Yourself:
Survivors of narcissistic abuse often find that their sense of success and achievement was shaped by the expectations of their abuser. Now, it's time to redefine what success means to you. Success could be measured in personal growth, emotional balance, or new achievements in your career, hobbies, or relationships. It's about finding fulfillment on your own terms, without external validation.

Trying New Things:
A significant part of moving forward is stepping out of your comfort zone and trying new things that inspire you. This could be exploring a new career path, learning a new skill, or even making changes in your lifestyle. By exploring new opportunities, you open yourself up to possibilities that can bring joy, personal growth, and a renewed sense of purpose. Taking risks can feel intimidating, but it also presents the chance to rediscover your strengths and passions.

Saying Yes to New Relationships and Connections:
Living authentically also involves surrounding yourself with people who align with your values and respect your boundaries. It's about creating relationships—whether romantic, platonic, or professional—that uplift and inspire you. By seeking out relationships rooted in mutual respect, trust, and understanding, you create a supportive network that helps you continue your journey of self-discovery.

Authenticity: Living in Alignment with Your True Self

After years of being stifled by narcissistic abuse, reconnecting with your authentic self is key to moving forward. Living authentically means embracing who you are—your strengths, vulnerabilities, passions, and values—and building a life that reflects this self-awareness.

Self-Discovery: Reconnecting with Your True Values and Desires:
During the healing process, it's important to engage in self-reflection and rediscover the values and desires that may have been overshadowed during the abusive relationship. Journaling, meditation, and therapy are effective tools for getting back in touch with the core aspects of yourself that you may have lost sight of. Ask yourself: What makes me feel alive? What do I genuinely enjoy? What are my core beliefs and values? By answering these questions, you can begin building a life that feels more authentic and fulfilling.

Practicing Authenticity in Everyday Life:
Living authentically requires daily practice. This means consistently aligning your actions and decisions with your true self, rather than the expectations of others. It involves listening to your intuition and honoring your needs. Whether it's speaking up in a meeting, expressing your preferences in a relationship, or pursuing a dream you've put on hold, practicing authenticity brings you closer to a life that feels truly your own.

Resilience in the Face of Adversity: Navigating Future Challenges

Although you've made great strides in healing, challenges may still arise. Living authentically also means accepting that setbacks are part of the journey and learning how to navigate them with resilience.

Resilience as a Lifelong Practice:
Resilience doesn't mean avoiding adversity—it means facing challenges with the strength and tools you've developed throughout your healing journey. Whether you encounter new difficulties in relationships, work, or personal life, it's essential to remember that you have the inner resources to handle them. Practicing mindfulness, self-care, and self-compassion helps you remain grounded, even during difficult times.

Adapting to Change:
Life is full of unexpected twists and turns, and as you continue to evolve, it's important to remain adaptable. Whether you're faced with external changes or internal growth, being open to adaptation allows you to navigate life's unpredictability with grace. By

maintaining flexibility, you create room for continued personal growth and transformation.

Celebrating Your Journey and Looking Ahead

Living authentically also means recognizing the progress you've made. This chapter encourages you to look back at how far you've come—from surviving narcissistic abuse to reclaiming your life and identity—and celebrate your resilience.

Acknowledging Your Achievements:
It's important to regularly acknowledge and celebrate your achievements, no matter how small. Whether it's setting a boundary in a relationship, achieving a personal goal, or simply feeling more confident in your daily life, these accomplishments reflect the strength and resilience you've cultivated. By celebrating these moments, you reinforce your ability to continue moving forward with confidence.

Looking Toward the Future with Optimism:
Your journey toward healing has been challenging, but it has also opened the door to a future filled with possibility. By living authentically and embracing the freedom to define your own path, you can look ahead with optimism, knowing that you have the strength and wisdom to face whatever comes next. This chapter encourages you to dream boldly, live fully, and continue evolving as you step into the future.

Conclusion: Living Authentically and Embracing Your Power

Chapter 12 serves as a final reminder that the journey of healing from narcissistic abuse doesn't end with recovery—it continues as you step into a life of authenticity, empowerment, and self-discovery. By letting go of the past, embracing new opportunities, and living in alignment with your true self, you can forge a future that reflects your values and aspirations.

Living authentically means trusting yourself, taking risks, and embracing your strengths. It means defining success on your own terms and surrounding yourself with relationships that honor who you are. As you continue on this path, remember that setbacks are part of the journey, but your resilience will carry you through.

This chapter—and this book—ends with the belief that every survivor has the power to not only recover but to thrive. By embracing authenticity, celebrating your progress, and looking forward with optimism, you have the tools to build a life that is truly your own. You are no longer defined by the abuse you endured—you are defined by the strength, wisdom, and power you've gained along the way.

Embracing Your Power as a Lifelong Journey

As you move forward from the challenges of narcissistic abuse, it's important to remember that empowerment is not a one-time event—it's a lifelong journey. The steps you've taken to reclaim your life, establish boundaries, and nurture your authentic self are part of an ongoing process of growth and self-discovery. Every decision you make to prioritize your well-being, every relationship you build on trust and respect, and every moment you take to celebrate your progress are reflections of your resilience and strength.

This journey is yours, and it's important to recognize that while you may face new obstacles, you now have the tools and knowledge to navigate them. Your healing has equipped you with the ability to advocate for yourself, embrace opportunities that align with your true self, and continue evolving in ways that bring you joy and fulfillment.

The Ripple Effect of Living Authentically

Living authentically doesn't just transform your own life—it has a ripple effect on those around you. By showing up as your true self, you inspire others to do the same. Your courage to heal, set boundaries, and pursue your passions empowers the people in your life to embrace their own authenticity. Whether in friendships, family relationships, or professional settings, your commitment to living with integrity and self-respect influences the dynamics around you, creating healthier, more supportive environments.

You also contribute to a larger movement of breaking free from toxic patterns and encouraging healthier relationships in the world. As you continue to grow and share your experiences, you become a beacon of hope for others who are still navigating their healing journeys. By living authentically, you give others permission to do the same, fostering a community of empowered individuals who are dedicated to mutual respect, compassion, and self-growth.

Giving Back: Turning Your Journey into a Source of Strength for Others

One of the most fulfilling aspects of the healing journey is the opportunity to give back. Many survivors of narcissistic abuse find that sharing their stories and offering support to others brings a sense of purpose and meaning to their recovery. Whether through mentoring, volunteering, or simply being there for someone who is starting their journey, your experiences can become a powerful source of inspiration for others.

Mentorship and Advocacy:
If you feel called to help others who have experienced abuse, consider becoming a mentor or advocate. Support groups, online forums, and nonprofit organizations often seek individuals with lived experience to guide others through their recovery. Your insights and empathy can provide much-needed encouragement and hope for those who feel lost or overwhelmed.

Volunteering and Community Engagement:
Giving back doesn't have to be directly related to your personal experience with abuse. Many survivors find healing through community service, using their time and talents to help others in various capacities. Whether it's working with youth, volunteering at a local shelter, or contributing to a cause that aligns with your values, giving back can reinforce your sense of purpose and connection to the world.

Creative Expression as a Tool for Healing:
For some, art, writing, or music becomes a powerful way to process and share their journey. Creative expression not only helps you continue healing but can also inspire others who may relate to your story. Whether it's through personal blogs, memoirs, or artistic projects, using creativity to reflect on your experiences can have a profound impact on both your healing process and those who encounter your work.

Living a Life Rooted in Your Values

At the heart of living authentically is staying true to your core values. After surviving narcissistic abuse, your priorities may have shifted, and what once seemed important may no longer hold the same meaning. This chapter encourages you to constantly reassess your values, ensuring that the choices you make are in alignment with the person you are today.

Building a Value-Based Life:
Whether it's in your career, relationships, or personal growth, grounding your decisions in your values allows you to live with intention. This creates a strong foundation for fulfillment and happiness. Your values act as a compass, guiding you through life's uncertainties and helping you make choices that support your well-being and personal growth.

Setting New Intentions for the Future:
As you continue your journey, take the time to set new intentions for the future. These intentions don't have to be rigid goals—they can be flexible guides that remind you of the kind of life you want to lead. Intentions might include commitments to self-care, seeking new experiences, cultivating joy, or continuing to build meaningful relationships. By keeping your intentions in mind, you can stay focused on living a life that honors your authentic self.

Embracing Peace and Joy in Everyday Life

The ultimate goal of healing is not just survival but thriving—and that includes embracing peace, joy, and contentment in your daily life. After years of enduring emotional manipulation and control, you deserve to experience happiness and fulfillment in all areas of life. Whether it's through small moments of mindfulness, spending time with loved ones, or pursuing your passions, allowing yourself to embrace joy is one of the greatest acts of self-love.

Gratitude as a Daily Practice:
One of the simplest yet most transformative practices for cultivating peace is gratitude. Taking time each day to reflect on the things you're grateful for—no matter how small—can shift your perspective and bring a sense of peace. Gratitude helps you focus on the positive

aspects of your life, reinforcing the progress you've made and the blessings you've encountered along the way.

Finding Joy in the Present Moment:
Living authentically means finding joy in the present, even amidst life's challenges. It's about being fully engaged in the moment, appreciating the beauty and wonder around you. By practicing mindfulness and staying present, you allow yourself to savor the small pleasures of life, from a quiet walk in nature to meaningful conversations with loved ones.

Conclusion: Stepping Boldly Into Your Future

As you reach the final chapter of this book, remember that your healing journey is ongoing. Every day presents new opportunities for growth, learning, and self-discovery. You have walked through the challenges of narcissistic abuse and come out stronger, wiser, and more empowered. Now, it's time to step boldly into your future with confidence, knowing that you have the tools, resilience, and inner strength to thrive.

You are no longer defined by your past or the trauma you've endured. You are defined by the courage you've shown, the wisdom you've gained, and the life you are creating. Embrace the power of your authenticity, continue to trust in your ability to navigate whatever comes your way, and always remember that your future is as bright and limitless as you choose to make it.

This chapter, and the book as a whole, leaves you with a final message: You are enough, just as you are. You are worthy of love, respect, joy, and fulfillment. And most importantly, you have the power to create a life that is truly your own—one filled with peace, purpose, and boundless possibility.

Conclusion

This book has explored the deeply personal and often painful journey of recovering from narcissistic abuse. At its heart, the message emphasizes the critical role of **awareness**—understanding the signs and tactics of narcissistic behavior, such as gaslighting, is the first crucial step toward regaining control. Awareness helps survivors recognize the patterns of manipulation they have endured, allowing them to gain clarity and empowerment in their recovery.

Dr. Judith Herman's pioneering research on **Complex PTSD (C-PTSD)** has shed light on the profound and long-lasting psychological effects that prolonged abuse can have. Through real-life stories, such as those of Michelle and John, we've seen how survivors can draw strength from supportive communities and professional guidance. Their experiences underscore the importance of a robust support network, whether through therapy, support groups, or online connections.

Another key theme is the importance of **setting boundaries**. Dr. Ramani Durvasula stresses that learning to say no and prioritizing self-care are critical for maintaining emotional well-being. Tools such as daily affirmations, journaling, and engaging in creative outlets like painting or traveling can significantly enhance self-esteem and emotional resilience.

Throughout the book, the role of **self-love and self-compassion** has been highlighted as essential components of the healing process. Cultivating a positive relationship with oneself allows survivors to rebuild their self-worth and regain autonomy, free from the shadows of their abusive past.

Erik Johnson

www.ingramcontent.com/pod-product-compliance
Lightning Source LLC
Chambersburg PA
CBHW072136070526
44585CB00016B/1701